The Book of the CORONATION PACIFICS

A Photographic Accompaniment: 2

By

Ian Sixsmith

IRWELL PRESS Ltd.

ISBN 1-903266-54-8

Cover photographs: a Polmadie Coronation, 46230 DUCHESS OF BUCCLEUCH at its home shed alongside 0-4-4T 55146 (J. Robertson, The Transport Treasury) and a Camden example out on the road, 46240 CITY OF COVENTRY approaching Shap summit with the down Royal Scot (coal pusher in use) on 5 September 1957 (Peter Groom).

First published in the United Kingdom in 2005
by Irwell Press Limited, 59A, High Street, Clophill,
Bedfordshire MK45 4BE
Printed by Newnorth, Bedford

Picture This

Readers by now familiar with these volumes will hardly need to read on, and can pass directly to the photographs but some explanation is necessary for New Boys. Over the last eight years or so the Irwell Press 'Book Of' locomotive studies (solid, hardback, anything from 96 pages to 200+ pages, depending on the class) has covered many of the principal BR express classes. Some have been reprinted while others are out of print; others remain to be reprinted. Beginning in 1997 they have been:

The Book of the BR Standards
The Book of the Coronation Pacifics
The Book of the Royal Scots
The Book of the Merchant Navy Pacifics
The Book of the Jubilee 4-6-0s
The Book of the West Country/Battle of Britain Pacifics
The Book of the Princess Royal Pacifics
The Book of the Patriot 4-6-0s
The Book of the BR Standards: 2
The Book of the A3 Pacifics
The Book of the Britannias

Next, there were the first paperback 'supplements' *The Book of the Britannias, A Photographic Accompaniment* and *The Book of the Coronation Pacifics, A Photographic Accompaniment:1.* Their purpose was to serve up a wider range of photographs for that particular class. On the way are suitable 'Accompaniments' for each of the locomotive classes in the series but this third one is devoted once again to the Stanier Coronations (or Princess

LIVERY CHANGES

No	First Livery	War. black	Exp. grey	LMS black	BR black	BR blue	BR green	BR red
6220	Blue	3/44	-	10/46	-	1/50	8/52	-
6221	Blue	8/44	-	7/46	-	2/50*	1/52	-
6222	Blue	10/44	-	5/46	-	9/50*	12/52	-
6223	Blue	2/44	-	8/46	-	3/50	9/52	-
6224	Blue	10/44	-	7/46	-	5/48#	4/52	-
6225	Red	4/44	-	3/47	-	2/50	2/53	8/58
6226	Red	?/44	-	6/47	11/48	5/49	4/51*	11/58
6227	Red	1/44	-	3/47	-	5/48#	5/53	-
6228	Red	4/44	-	11/47	-	8/50	8/55	6/58
6229	Red	8/43*	-	12/47	-	1/50*	3/52	9/58
6230	Red	-	-	9/46	-	5/48#	3/52	-
6231	Red	8/45*	-	9/46	-	5/48#	11/53	-
6232	Red	2/45	-	9/47	-	-	11/51*	-
6233	Red	-	-	9/46	-	-	12/52*	-
6234	Red	-	3/46	-	-	5/48#	1/52	-
6235	Red	3/43	-	4/46	-	10/50*	4/53	-
6236	Red	4/44	-	12/47	-	-	8/55	7/58
6237	Red	8/43*	-	2/47	-	8/49*	8/52*	-
6238	Red	?/43	-	8/46	3/49	-	10/53	6/58
6239	Red	3/44*	-	9/47	-	6/50*	7/54*	-
6240	Red	11/45	-	7/47	-	1/50	9/54*	7/58
6241	Red	5/43*	-	2/47	-	5/48#	4/53*	-
6242	Red	5/44	-	5/47	-	8/49	11/53	-
6243	Red	1/44	-	-	-	6/49	1/54*	10/58
6244	Red	1/44	-	8/47	-	9/48#	5/53	10/58
6245	Black	New	-	11/47	-	-	4/53	12/57
6246	Black	New	-	11/46	11/48	-	5/53*	10/58
6247	Black	New	-	2/47	-	-	1/54*	5/58
6248	Black	New	-	1/47	3/49	-	8/53*	6/58
6249	Black	New	-	11/46	-	8/50*	1/53*	-
6250	Black	New	-	7/47	-	3/50*	9/52*	-
6251	Black	New	-	6/47	4/49	-	10/51*	11/58
6252	Black	New	-	11/46*	3/49	?/50	1/54*	-
6253	Black	-	-	New	-	-	10/53*	-
6254	Black	-	-	New	-	8/50*	1/53**	9/58
6255	Black	-	-	New	-	6/50	4/53	-
6256	Black	-	-	New	11/48	3/51*	5/54*	5/58
6257	Black	-	-	-	New	-	11/52*	-

*Table adapted from Rowledge (*The LMS Pacifics, *D&C 1987), with kind permission.*
*approximate—probably into service some weeks later
#'experimental' blue when first painted
**This date appeared in 'The Book Of' and in the British Railways Illustrated Coronation Special of August 2001. Graham Onley's fading memories, bolstered by recent correspondence in the railway press, suggest 46254 retained blue until 1954... 46236, 46256 and 46257 ran with tenders lettered BRITISH RAILWAYS

CORONATION as a 'semi', with the up Royal Scot running through Norton Bridge in 1953. Attempts to improve the mileages of the Polmadie Coronations included working them through to London on the Royal Scot in summer some years – 1953 was obviously such a year. In truth the Pacifics were only ever allocated to Polmadie for political reasons, for there was no logic in having them there and then only using them between Glasgow and Carlisle!

Coronations, Duchesses, 'semis' 'big 'uns', call them what you will). It accompanies, supplements and complements the second 'Book Of', *The Book of the Coronation Pacifics* by Ian Sixsmith, first published in 1998, subsequently reprinted twice and long out of print – until now.

****

I would like to thank Eric Youldon, Barry Hoper, Peter Rowledge, Richard Derry, Allan Baker, John Corkill, Bryan Wilson, Graham Onley and Martin Smith in compiling this pictorial.

In Brief

The previous volumes covered the design, development and history, as well as providing the 'engine-picking' guide to these remarkable locomotives. So apart from a brief resume of their construction it's 'straight to the photographs'...

SOME DETAILS

Loco	To traffic	S/C	Tender No.	DC	SD added	SB restored
46220	6/37	S	9703	12/44	9/46	12/55
46221	6/37	S	9704	11/40	5/46	9/52
46222	6/37	S	9705	8/43	5/46	8/53
46223	7/37	S	9706	11/41	8/46	8/55
46224	7/37	S	9707	5/40	5/46	10/54
46225	5/38	S	9743	6/43	2/47	1/55
46226	5/38	S	9744	7/42	6/47	11/55
46227	6/38	S	9745	12/40	2/47	5/53
46228	6/38	S	9746	9/40	7/47	1/57
46229	9/38	S	9747	4/43	11/47	2/57
46230	6/38	C	9748	10/40	9/46	-
46231	6/38	C	9749	6/40	9/46	-
46232	7/38	C	9750	1/43	2/45	-
46233	7/38	C	9751	3/41	9/46	-
46234	8/38	C	9752	2/39	3/46	-
46235	7/39	S	9798	New	4/46	7/52
46236	7/39	S	9799	New	12/47	11/53
46237	8/39	S	9800	New	1/47	5/56
46238	9/39	S	9801	New	11/46	10/53
46239	9/39	S	9802	New	6/47	2/57
46240	3/40	S	9803	New	6/47	5/57
46241	4/40	S	9804	New	1/47	2/58
46242	5/40	S	9805	New	3/47	11/53
46243	6/40	S	9806	New	5/49	11/58
46244	7/40	S	9807	New	8/47	7/53
46245	6/43	S	9808	New	8/47	12/57
46246	8/43	S	9809	New	9/46	5/60
46247	9/43	S	9810	New	5/47	5/58
46248	10/43	S	9811	New	12/46	6/58
46249	4/44	C	9812	New	11/46	-
46250	5/44	C	9813	New	3/46	-
46251	6/44	C	9814	New	8/46	-
46252	6/44	C	9815	New	3/45	
46253	9/46	C	9816	New	New	-
46254	9/46	C	9817	New	New	-
46255	10/46	C	10622	New	New	-
46256	12/47	C	10623	New	New	-
46257	5/48	C	10624	New	New	-

S = Streamliner
C = Conventional
SD = Smoke Deflector
SB = Smokebox
DC = Double Chimney

An impression of how the streamliners looked in 1938 with the Coronation Scot streamliner train. On the right 6220 CORONATION (you can't see the number but the crown above the nameplate gives it away; the name commemorated GEORGE VI's Coronation of 1937) is pounding up Camden bank while below another (it looks like 6223 PRINCESS ALICE) is storming through Rugby. The voluptuous curving of the front of the locomotives seemed not to have the striking quality of the rival LNER's A4s (though all this is in the eye of the beholder of course). However, from the front, as here, any suggestion of 'bulbousness' fell away. CORONATION on 29 June 1937 had run the celebrated trial train for the gentlemen of the press from Euston to Crewe. It was at a spot some two miles short of Crewe that the train famously touched 114mph and made the record (for a while). It was a near thing, astonishingly so – it would probably lead to a mass-gaoling today... H.A.V. Bulleid in *Master Builders of Steam* (Ian Allan, 1963) describes how F.A. Lemon, sat with Stanier, braced his legs on the seat opposite in anticipation of the wreck. Stanier, in true insouciant leader style, remained calm and collected – he later declared that they had been saved from disaster by the de Glehn bogie.

1937: 6220-6224
6220 CORONATION
6221 QUEEN ELIZABETH
6222 QUEEN MARY
6223 PRINCESS ALICE
6224 PRINCESS ALEXANDRA
All streamlined

1938: 6225-6234
6225 DUCHESS OF GLOUCESTER
6226 DUCHESS OF NORFOLK
6227 DUCHESS OF DEVONSHIRE
6228 DUCHESS OF RUTLAND
6229 DUCHESS OF HAMILTON
All streamlined

6230 DUCHESS OF BUCCLEUCH
6231 DUCHESS OF ATHOLL
6232 DUCHESS OF MONTROSE
6233 DUCHESS OF SUTHERLAND
6234 DUCHESS OF ABERCORN
All non-streamlined

1939: 6235-6239
6235 CITY OF BIRMINGHAM
6236 CITY OF BRADFORD
6237 CITY OF BRISTOL
6238 CITY OF CARLISLE
6239 CITY OF CHESTER
All streamlined

1940: 6240-6244
6240 CITY OF COVENTRY
6241 CITY OF EDINBURGH
6242 CITY OF GLASGOW
6243 CITY OF LANCASTER
6244 CITY OF LEEDS (renamed KING GEORGE VI April 1941)
All streamlined

1943: 6245-6248
6245 CITY OF LONDON
6246 CITY OF MANCHESTER
6247 CITY OF LIVERPOOL
6248 CITY OF LEEDS
All streamlined

1944: 6249-6252
6249 CITY OF SHEFFIELD
6250 CITY OF LICHFIELD
6251 CITY OF NOTTINGHAM
6252 CITY OF LEICESTER
All non-streamlined

1946-48: 6253-6257
6253 CITY OF ST ALBANS
6254 CITY OF STOKE-ON-TRENT
6255 CITY OF HEREFORD
6256 SIR WILLIAM A. STANIER, F.R.S.
6257 CITY OF SALFORD
All non-streamlined

To complete this very, very brief introduction, we really need 'An Official'. This is 6225 DUCHESS OF GLOUCESTER in the traditional works grey, applied to highlight the detail. In both *The Book of the Coronation Pacifics* and the *Accompaniment:1* attention was drawn to the unfortunate habit the LMS had of swopping the identities of locomotives to be photographed. It was easier to alter the plates and numbers rather than paint and prepare every one in turn! See for instance, page 18 in *The Book of the Coronation Pacifics.* Inevitably some got out of sequence and we get matches of names to numbers that never were, though DUCHESS OF GLOUCESTER here is apparently 'real'. The picture is useful for some of the typical features – the hollow axles, fluted motion, the flimsy front step, ventilating louvres behind the buffers which only appeared after the first batch of five, three sandbox fillers feeding the front of the leading driver and front and rear of the middle one but not the rear wheel; prominent worksplate, the bracket for the Stone-Deuta 'speedo', the cowlings front and aft on the tender and the sliding door to get the 'bag' in when taking water. Particularly prominent are the holes in the casing for the firebox washout plugs.

46221 QUEEN ELIZABETH dropping off vans at Penrith about 1962 – these were of course fading times for the 'big 'uns' though, oddly, across some parts of the country they were more readily seen than before. Duties such as these brought them out in daylight more! Crewe North ones especially (QUEEN ELIZABETH might still be based at Crewe North in this view, for she didn't go to Upperby until 1962) were traditionally to be found 'on nights' with sleepers and so on to Glasgow and Perth. Photograph J. Robertson, The Transport Treasury.

A glittering green Polmadie 46221 QUEEN ELIZABETH with the Royal Scot at Beattock, 2 May 1953. The characteristic sleeper fence was there to prevent drifting snow. Photograph J. Robertson, The Transport Treasury.

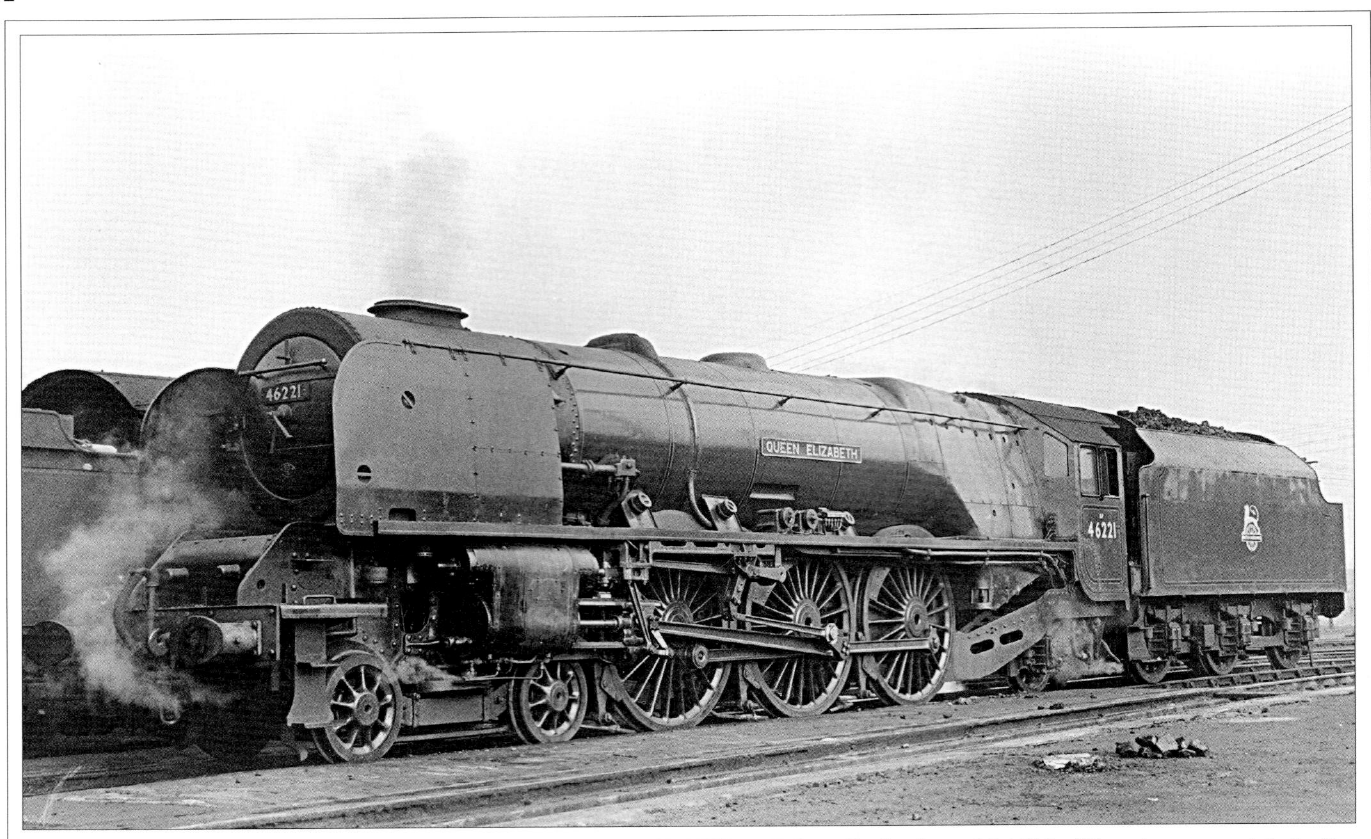

Power personified. A green liveried 46221 QUEEN ELIZABETH at Polmadie in the mid-1950s. The strange notch in the boiler cladding, as pointed out elsewhere in these columns, was made to clear the lids of the lubricators on the running plate. It's useful to compare this view with a very similar one in *The Book of the Coronation Pacifics* page iv; in it, QUEEN ELIZABETH takes up a similar stance but is in 'semi' state (with small cab window, unlike here) and an earlier 'mixed' livery. The sand fillers were very prominent on the Coronations and the lids were normally of this type, with a diagonal 'rib'. Earlier ones (see particularly *The Book of the Jubilee 4-6-0s*) had lids with a simple 'knob' in the middle; the picture in *The Book of the Coronation Pacifics* shows 46221 to have picked up both types, which is quite unusual. By the time of this picture, all are 'ribbed'. How's that for 'engine picking'? And if that doesn't get you to buy 'The Book Of...' Photograph The Transport Treasury.

QUEEN MARY as a 'semi' (a term scarcely appropriate to her royal station) at Dundee in early BR days; renumbered but still with LMS on the tender, in a sort of relict (with added grime) 1946 black livery. Note larger cab windows on both engines on this page compared, say, to the various streamliners.

46222 QUEEN MARY at Crewe North shed in BR green, 22 April 1955. It was a Polmadie engine more or less for its entire life and thus seldom to be found in London. Photograph Peter Groom.

46222 QUEEN MARY waits at Crewe with an extra van on 6 August 1958, ready to take over the Birmingham-Glasgow train. 'Speedo' newly fitted. Photograph Alec Swain, The Transport Treasury.

46222 QUEEN MARY ex-works at Crewe on 8 November 1959. Like QUEEN ELIZABETH earlier, a 'compare and contrast' exercise with *The Book of the Coronation Pacifics* (page 16) will probably turn out to be rewarding, from the livery changes, smokebox and even the toecap notch on the smoke deflector to the sand filler lids and the Polmadie shed plate – from 27A to 66A! The 'speedo' (see previous page) has been repaired/renewed.

6223 PRINCESS ALICE (single chimney, note) with the up Coronation Scot, passing Acton Bridge about 1939. It is worth noting the prominent rim at the base of the streamlined tender, part of the streamlining which disappeared when the engines were 'conventionalised'. For the next few years large parts of the population would dream of a plump chicken like that one, striding around the grass at the edge of the line... Photograph Rail Archive Stephenson.

As pointed out in *The Book of the Coronation Pacifics, A Photographic Accompaniment:1*, where 46223 PRINCESS ALICE is shown at this same spot but in a rather earlier era, she was another long-term Polmadie engine, spending most of her working life there. So, while it was one of the Scottish rarities south of Crewe (depending on the year and the time of year), to a local spotter at Glasgow it would be the umpteenth sighting. The lovely lamps shown in *Photographic Accompaniment:1* have given way to the illuminated boxes on concrete posts in this view a year later on 7 July 1957. Photograph A.E. Bennett.

The Coronation Scot behind 6224 PRINCESS ALEXANDRA 'somewhere on the route', in 1938/39. The joins in the casing weathered poorly and the staining, particularly at the edging around the doors, is clear. Photograph The Transport Treasury.

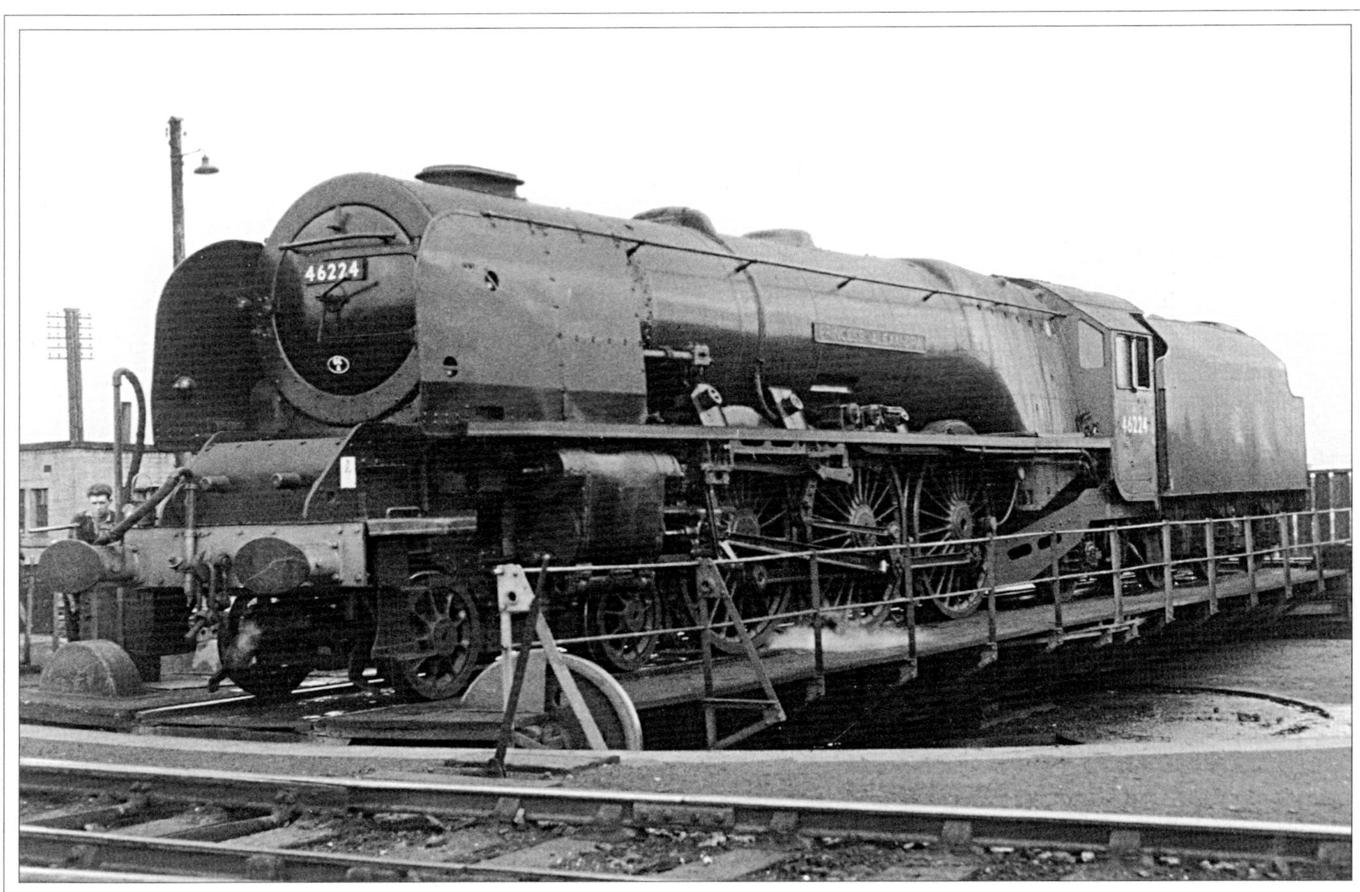

All the first five Coronations, the 'blue and white' streamliners spent years at Polmadie – none more than PRINCESS ALEXANDRA. Here she is on the Polmadie turntable, in green in the late 1950s and in an unusual combination for a BR express locomotive; she already has the electrification flashes (newly applied by the look of them) which began to appear on the LM in 1959 and also the 'speedo' but AWS has yet to show. 46224 PRINCESS ALEXANDRA was odd in other ways, suffering two of the worst misfortunes to befall the 'big 'uns'. Most noteworthy was a violent explosion and the scalding to death of the unfortunate Fireman, when the firebox crown was exposed on the climb to Craigenhill on 10 September 1940. The incident was ascribed to wartime conditions, with the big engine put into the hands of an inexperienced crew. Bizarrely, the same engine sustained another crown collapse, on 5 March 1948, at Lamington only twelve miles or so from the scene of the first disaster! This time the Driver it was who was killed, and he had had long experience of the Coronations. Photograph J. Robertson, The Transport Treasury.

46225 DUCHESS OF GLOUCESTER at work as a 'semi' in April 1952, leaving Preston with an up train. It emerged with a conventional smokebox at the beginning of 1955.

46225 DUCHESS OF GLOUCESTER at Polmadie ready for the Mid-Day Scot, a job jealously guarded by Crewe North. Note the lime deposits on the cylinder casing. You do see this on Coronations, but not often. Photograph Hamish Stevenson.

46225 DUCHESS OF GLOUCESTER passes Lamington with the 12.20pm Perth-Euston on 1 August 1964. This beautiful locomotive, first of the 'golden' batch and the first of the 'Duchess' series, was withdrawn only a few weeks later. Was it ever photographed next to 'husband' 71000? What a picture that would have made... Photograph W.A.C. Smith.

More moorland, with 46226 DUCHESS OF NORFOLK heading a mix of vans and coaches. The location is the last half mile to Beattock summit, near Upper Howecleuch at about 1,100ft. The train is W27 (later IS53), the 9.25am Crewe to Perth which always had vans marshalled next to the engine, and sometimes horseboxes too. The locomotive on this job north of Carlisle should have been a Polmadie Britannia (one of their few jobs) off the 7am Glasgow Central-Carlisle. The 9.25am Crewe-Perth was a strange animal in that from Crewe to Carlisle it had the Polmadie Duchess off the 11.15pm Glasgow-Birmingham (to Crewe) of the previous night which came off at Carlisle to be replaced by the Britannia – one Polmadie loco off for another. The Duchess finished up on the 2.10pm all stations Carlisle-Glasgow Central. Photograph Derek Cross.

46227 DUCHESS OF DEVONSHIRE as a 'semi', on the down Royal Scot passing Carstairs in 1952. The Duchesses proper (though the name was frequently accorded to the class as a whole) were the ten engines built in 1938, the first five streamlined, the second five conventional. The naming policy then changed to cities. This probably got a better return in terms of PR, because there was no shortage of suitable nobility. As pointed out in *The Book of the Coronation Pacifics*, the Duchess of York would have been perfect or even the Duchess of Bedford for that matter.

No express passenger locomotives in Great Britain had a more stately and impressive appearance than these massive machines. So wrote Cecil J. Allen wrote in *British Pacific Locomotives* (Ian Allan, 1962) and he could have had this view of 46227 DUCHESS OF DEVONSHIRE at Preston with a Manchester Victoria-Glasgow train in mind, in July 1961. Photograph D. Beecroft, The Transport Treasury.

6228 DUCHESS OF RUTLAND with the up Royal Scot at Acton Bridge about 1938-39. This is a 'red one' of course in the sumptuous red and gold. This wore better than the blue which, as BR was still finding out thirty years later, stood up poorly to working conditions and suffered premature fading and streaking. Photograph Rail Archive Stephenson.

46228 DUCHESS OF RUTLAND, back in red and in near perfect nick at Crewe Works, 22 June 1958. It has just had a 'Heavy Intermediate' lasting several weeks and has obviously had attention in the Paint Shop (behind). The shine on the engine is so good it sparkles even on a rainy day. 'Speedo' fitted but no AWS or electrification flashes. Photograph Gerald Adams, John Stretton Collection.

In what could hardly be more of a contrast, DUCHESS OF RUTLAND traces its way through Crewe with an up parcels, September 1963. Photograph C. Martin, The Transport Treasury.

A fine-looking 46229 DUCHESS OF HAMILTON with the 2.10pm Euston-Liverpool leaving Beechwood tunnel between Coventry and Birmingham, diverted from the Trent Valley main line on Sunday 25 June 1961. DUCHESS OF HAMILTON, of course, was Billy Butlin's engine for his Minehead camp and it spent over ten years there. It certainly got to some strange places; most notably the United States, for 6229 it was which went in 1939 disguised as CORONATION. It returned across a dangerous Atlantic to go back into traffic in March 1942. It was not repaired and restored to its Duchess persona until the following year, so the two must have ran 'swopped' in Britain for some time. The reasons for the switch (CORONATION merely donated its plates and numbers and took up 6229's identity) was that the PR people deemed a red and gold engine would yield more PR 'oomph' in America. Photograph Michael Mensing.

A justly familiar and justly celebrated portrait, 46229 DUCHESS OF HAMILTON photographed from the shed roof at Edge Hill by photographer/Fireman Jim Carter. Edge Hill gained a small stud of 8P Pacifics (Coronations and Princesses) to serve, in the main, as standbys for the uncertain EE Type 4s. During early 1962 they were allowed over the Liverpool-Wigan line, working through to Carlisle with a freight, though they rarely managed the booked return working. Their standby duties were extended to Lime Street-Glasgow Central sleeper but the Pacifics were got rid of while problems persisted with the EE Type 4s. Their continued failures then had to be covered by Britannias and even Black Fives. Photograph Jim Carter.

Pleasing traditional portrait of long-time Polmadie stalwart 46230 DUCHESS OF BUCCLEUCH with the Royal Scot at Beattock, 22 August 1952. It was the first of the engines built without streamlining. Photograph J. Robertson, The Transport Treasury.

46230 DUCHESS OF BUCCLEUCH passing Lugton Junction with the 5.30pm Glasgow St Enoch to Carlisle, 23 April 1960. Photograph W.A.C. Smith.

46231 DUCHESS OF ATHOLL at Polmadie on 4 November 1951, on one of the roads ending at the brick wall 'out the back'. The smoke deflectors here (as in many other illustrations in these books) have yet to have the notch cut at the base, at the join with the running plate where it tapered almost to nothing. It was done to give more room for a cleaner's toe cap. 46231 was another Coronation involved in a fatal accident, the Ecclefechan collision of 21 July 1945 which killed both Driver and Fireman. Photographs James Stevenson, courtesy Hamish Stevenson.

46231 DUCHESS OF ATHOLL with Jubilee 45631 TANGANYIKA leading, at Northampton with the 10.20 Euston-Liverpool on 28 January 1962. Photograph John Edgington.

Euston arrival, and the classic Platform No.1 scene, pristine 46232 DUCHESS OF MONTROSE having arrived with the Royal Scot at teatime, 30 July 1952. It was still sunny outside and the engine seems to have brought some of it in with it. This is quite a photograph – two Glasgow engines in London at once! If Polmadie Pacifics habitually came off at Carlisle, nonetheless there were periods when they regularly worked through to London with the Royal Scot, in occasional short summer timetable periods, of which 1957 was one. It was an attempt to improve the mileage figures of the Polmadie ones which, many considered, would have been better employed (in the sense of having the opportunity to run more miles) in England. Alongside is 46102 BLACK WATCH, another Polmadie resident which by some miracle has found its way south on some sort of unbalanced working, to stand unexpectedly alongside its shedmate. Photograph J.C. Flemons, The Transport Treasury.

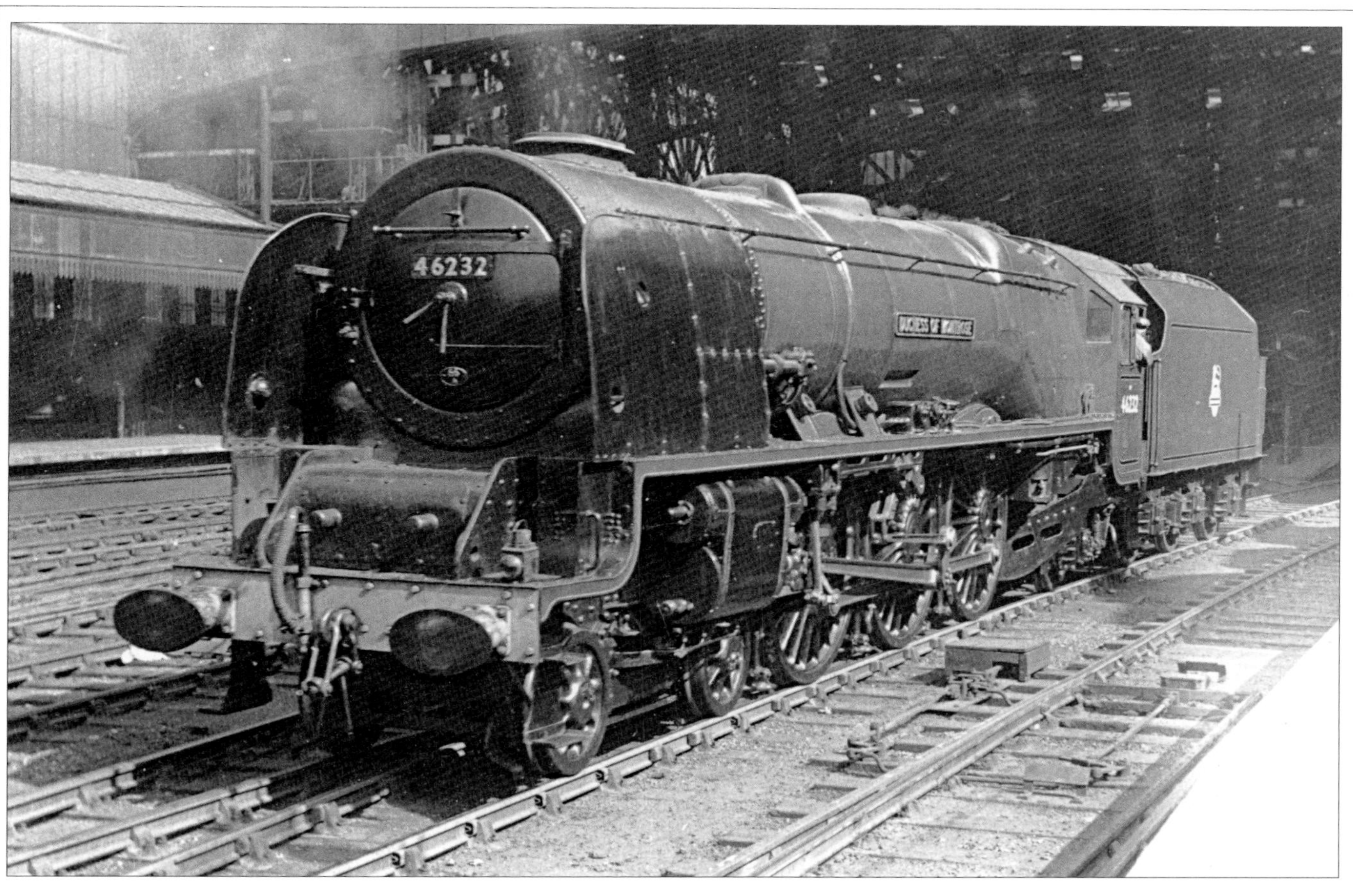

DUCHESS OF MONTROSE at Glasgow Central in the mid-1950s. With a name like that she could only be a long-time Scottish Coronation, though some thoroughly Scottish Duchesses stayed in England and vice-versa. DUCHESS OF MONTROSE was remarkable for surviving Nazi bombs which fell on Rose Lane bridge near Berkhamsted on 16 November 1940. J.W.P. Rowledge in *The LMS Pacifics* (an essential part of any 'big 'un' library, David & Charles, 1987) describes the incident briefly: 'a stick of bombs hit the bridge and as the girders fell the Duchess, with the 10am down from Euston, ran into them and was badly damaged. By a miracle there were no casualties and the engine was taken into Crewe Works two days later'. Photograph P.J. Sharpe, Norman Preedy Archive.

A Coronation without smoke deflectors, conventionally built 6233 DUCHESS OF SUTHERLAND (later installed by Sir Billy Butlin at his Heads of Ayr camp) in red with the shaded transfers, passing Acton Bridge in 1938/39. It was assumed, for some reason, that the big express engines would be mothballed for the duration of the coming war and a number were briefly transferred to outlying sheds rather after the fashion of protecting the national art treasures. They were quickly flung back into the fray of course and their enormous powers of haulage and endurance (despite the extra maintenance consequent upon the streamlined casing) proved an inestimable boon. Photograph Rail Archive Stephenson.

46233 DUCHESS OF SUTHERLAND on 1 August 1950. Oddly enough this Crewe North engine has been photographed at Balornock shed, or St Rollox as it was better known to latter-day enthusiasts. You don't see this very often. It would have worked to Perth from Crewe and then been filched for a job to Glasgow during the long layover before return to England. Photograph John Stretton Collection.

That characteristic brooding bulk – 46233 DUCHESS OF SUTHERLAND, one of two or three of them with stirring Scottish Duchess names never (see also above) to have been based at Polmadie. Photograph Gavin Morrison Collection.

46234 DUCHESS OF ABERCORN starting out from Shrewsbury in 1955, with a good profile of that noble double chimney. It was DUCHESS OF ABERCORN that demonstrated in awe-inspiring fashion the advantages of the double chimney and blastpipe, such that a whole section is devoted to it in *The Book of the Coronation Pacifics.* In trials in 1939 it took twenty coaches, over 600 tons, from Crewe to Glasgow and back; among the many superlatives was the attainment of over 2,500 drawbar horsepower – an unprecedented figure. All Coronations got to Shrewsbury regularly, either running in from Crewe or working through from Scotland/the north. Such engines would come off at Crewe and work forward (on a West of England train, perhaps) after servicing, but not turning, at Crewe North. They'd turn on the triangle at Shrewsbury and take a train back to Crewe where they'd then be 'right way round' for a job back north. Photograph The Transport Treasury.

46235 CITY OF BIRMINGHAM as a 'semi' (the first to be so transformed) at Crewe North; It had been resident there since 1944. Crewe North got Coronations early on, in 1938, though astonishingly they had to use the Gresty Lane - Sorting Sidings North triangle in the absence of a suitable turntable at the shed (though, if pressed, they did use the 70ft turntable at Crewe South). It was not until BR days, in 1950, that a new 70ft turntable came into use, part of an extensive modernisation scheme that was later drastically curtailed.

46235 CITY OF BIRMINGHAM, with AWS, runs into Bletchley in September 1961. The train, a good 'big 'un' loading, typically recedes into the far distance. Photograph J.A.C. Kirke, The Transport Treasury.

The results of the British Railways Locomotive Exchanges of 1948 have been pored over repeatedly down the years, most recently in a *British Railways Illustrated* Special. 46236 CITY OF BRADFORD, in 'semi' condition, was less scintillating than we might have hoped; on the Southern, for instance, the Pacific's driver was said to have been more concerned with coal consumption than dazzling performance. Here it is running light through Finsbury Park about 1pm on 29 April 1948, on its way to Camden for weekend maintenance. On its Southern trips it had a WD tender lettered LMS; this is shown in *The Book of the Coronation Pacifics* as well as *Accompaniment:1.* Photograph J.C. Flemons, The Transport Treasury.

CITY OF BRADFORD with The Caledonian, heading south past Winwick Junction, 21 August 1957. The Caledonian was a light loading for a Coronation but its introduction seems to have been the reason for painting some of them red. When someone realised that the Crewe and Polmadie ones tended to be engaged more on night work than the others the expensive repaintings were ended. What was the point of a new livery that no one would see? CITY OF BRADFORD, for the record, 'went red' in July 1958. Photograph Les Elsey.

Under The Wires: 1. CITY OF BRADFORD in latter-day guise; AWS-fitted, Carlisle Upperby shedplate, at Crewe under the new electrification about 1961. Photograph The Transport Treasury.

A 'blue 'un' on a Royal; a shimmering 46237 CITY OF BRISTOL awaits departure from Euston about 1950 with those four lamps up. Note the black buffers, black so they can't be marked. Part of series, similar views appear in both *The Book of the Coronation Pacifics* and *Accompaniment:1.* Photograph Alec Swain, The Transport Treasury.

46237 CITY OF BRISTOL in an unlikely role. Chosen for its name maybe, it was transferred to the Western Region for a four week period of trials in April 1955, to point the way, if possible, to reducing inconsistencies in the performance of the Kings. Amity was not the order of the day and no tangible or useful results seem to have flowed from the trials. The big Pacific was put on trains half the length the 'big 'uns' were used to and the first job, the nine coach Merchant Venturer to Bristol was changed when the Bath Road turntables proved too small. 46237 was then put on the Cornish Riviera and some Wolverhampton jobs. CITY OF BRISTOL soldiered on to the end, in September 1964; more than soldiered on in fact, for as late as the end of May it was reported on the Mid-Day Scot 'in immaculate condition'. Photograph M.W. Earley.

Under The Wires: 2. 46238 CITY OF CARLISLE in red livery rumbles through Crewe station to the delight of young and old alike on the platform, 25 July 1961. She has come off an up train and is backing out light to North shed. Photograph Alec Swain, The Transport Treasury.

CITY OF CARLISLE looking brilliant even in the summer rain, brilliant because it is immediately fresh from a Heavy in the new BR red, 22 June 1958. That GW-type dummy would suggest the location is Shrewsbury. 46238 was another one which operated to the end, in September 1964, and it is impossible not to conclude that the class was largely in good nick and capable of another year or two's work at the least. The problem was finding the right work of course. Take this entry in *The Railway Observer* describing CITY OF CARLISLE at Lancaster, on 29 May 1964: *At 19.40 46238 appeared on a down train consisting of two open passenger coaches, a restaurant car, three sleeping cars, about ten 'conflats' complete with containers, three open wagons containing bright yellow equipment and a goods brake!* The exclamation mark was well deserved. Photograph The Transport Treasury.

Under The Wires: 3. 46238 CITY OF CARLISLE with the down relief to the Sunday Royal Scot, just north of Shilton on 7 April 1963. The next year, on 4 September 1964, it would take the last down Caledonian from Crewe to Carlisle. As Rowledge puts it: 'surely that was arranged'! The last up train ran the same day, behind D212. Appropriately an Upperby engine at the last, it was taken out of service in mid-September and dumped with others in sidings at Upperby. Photograph Michael Mensing.

Inside Willesden roundhouse with a 1A plate, 46239 CITY OF CHESTER rests unused in early October 1963 after the exertions of the summer timetable in what was rapidly becoming a diesel depot. Its fine condition reflects the 'last fling' outlook of the Camden A/DMPS, John Fore. A highly unusual visitor the same day was the last B12, 61572, which was engaged about this time on the wildly circular 'Wandering 1500' tour on 5 October. See *Cheek by Jowl* in *British Railways Illustrated Vol.12 No.3*, December 2003. Photograph The Transport Treasury.

46240 CITY OF COVENTRY at Shrewsbury on a turn from Crewe (presumably after works attention) in the 1950s. The engine is in green with the first tender emblem; come 1958 it went into the BR red livery and would enjoy a celebrated swansong, along with its Willesden *confrere* 46245 CITY OF LONDON. Photograph The Transport Treasury.

46240 CITY OF COVENTRY at Willesden after its ejection from Camden (where it had served as the Royal engine for a while) by the diesel influx. It fairly luxuriated in red livery and certainly had plenty of extra care lavished on it. Here it is at Willesden shed on 7 July 1964 – a few weeks later it was transferred to Crewe North. It ranged far and wide to the end, turning up at Chester, for instance, at the end of March with a parcels train; by June, along with the equally well kept 46245, it could be found on Birmingham Newspaper trains and even the evening Tring-Stechford cement train! Photograph The Transport Treasury.

CITY OF COVENTRY out at work in those last years – they looked two or three power classes above the 7Ps rather than only one... Photograph The Transport Treasury.

46115

46241 CITY OF EDINBURGH at Rugby with the down Royal Scot, Whit Monday 26 May 1958. Despite the name it was never based in Scotland and had been a Camden engine for most of its life. It was one of the handful that found themselves at Edge Hill towards the end, mopping up for EE Type 4s that were failing, particularly with heating boiler problems in the dire winter of 1962-63. Three, 46229, 46241 and 46243, had gone to Edge Hill in March 1961. Photograph Michael Mensing.

46242 CITY OF GLASGOW, which was only ever briefly associated with Polmadie, runs into Euston with the prestige Caledonian on 25 April 1958. This could in fact be described as 'the thirty-ninth Coronation'; 46242 was all but destroyed in the terrible Harrow crash of 1952 and however Crewe might describe it as 'rebuilt' it was, in effect, a new engine. It famously emerged with the 'drape' of the running plate in front of the cylinders, as per the conventionally built ones 6230-6234 and 6249-6252. Photograph A.E. Bennett.

46243 CITY OF LANCASTER, in green livery and still a 'semi', at Polmadie with The Mid-Day Scot headboard, 14 May 1955. CITY OF LANCASTER was a solidly Crewe North engine and this train one of its prized jobs. As noted in the earlier *Book Of*, it was an out and home job and the only one in the Perth Link in which the crew saw daylight from the footplate in the winter months. The Perth Link was very special and men either took to the exceptional work like ducks to water or they found it extremely disagreeable. They could elect to skip it altogether for it was deliberately put aside from normal sequence of progression through the links—see Allan Baker and Gavin Morrison's *Crewe Sheds*, Ian Allan, 1988 and a wonderful read. Photograph J. Robertson, B.P. Hoper Collection.

46244 KING GEORGE VI in 'semi' condition at Shrewsbury in June 1954. The odd sloping smokebox was aesthetically a major distraction – the principal drawback was the exposure and undue emphasis on the chimney which looked completely out of kilter with the main body of the locomotive. Photograph The Transport Treasury.

46244 KING GEORGE VI takes the Wishaw South line at Law Junction with the 9.25am from Crewe to Perth, 27 May 1963. The engine will barely notice five coaches. Photograph W.A.C. Smith.

46245 CITY OF LONDON, one of the 'immaculate pair' (along with 46240) at Willesden at the end. Here it is at Euston, before Camden closed to steam, on 19 August 1961. Photograph T.J. Edgington.

There were a number of perambulations of Coronations across BR, from CITY OF BRADFORD on the Southern and even more outlandish places during the Exchanges, the trials with CITY OF BRISTOL on the Western to the later substitutions for the Kings as well as tours on the WR. Red-liveried 46245 CITY OF LONDON (see it in extended detail at Old Oak Common in *Accompaniment:1*) was in good condition to the end and thus a favourite for tours. One of its most notable 'foreign exploits', before application of the dreaded cabside stripe which so besmirched it on its WR work, took place on 9 June 1963 from Kings Cross; here is the wonderful beast ready to depart that day, at a curiously deserted platform. Note the four safety valves and the Stanier 'hooter'. Photograph Alistair Nisbet.

A Coronation on the Great Northern (cont.)

Its job that day, 9 June 1963, was a run down the GN main line from Kings Cross to Doncaster for the Works Open Day, in the last weeks of steam operation south of Peterborough. Here it waits to leave, amid a distinct lack of platform-end frenzy. Oddly, an appearance of stunning singularity had taken place only the day before, when a Holbeck Jubilee, 45597, good old BARBADOS, had found its way to the terminus (reported *The Railway Observer*). To any contemporary lineside observer this would have been an event on a par with Haley's Comet passing across the face of the sun while it was in eclipse, while Bristol City F.C. won the Premiership and FA Cup Double. For the third year running. Photograph Alistair Nisbet.

This fine broadside view shows CITY OF LONDON after arrival at Doncaster, on shed with B1 61157 in the background. Photograph The Transport Treasury.

A pristine 46246 CITY OF MANCHESTER at Crewe North, where it was resident throughout the entire decade of the 1950s. It was the last one to get a conventional smokebox, as late as 1960. Photograph R.K. Blencowe.

46246 CITY OF MANCHESTER departs from Rugby under the shadows of its own exhaust in February 1962. Photograph The Transport Treasury.

The Royal Scot gets underway from Glasgow Central behind 46247 CITY OF LIVERPOOL, 23 January 1960. Some eighteen months later, by the summer of 1961, there were sufficient Type 4 diesels (the first Peaks as well as the EE type 4s) for the three named Anglo-Scottish trains, Royal Scot, Mid-Day Scot and Caledonian, as well as some Perth trains, to be regularly diesel hauled; hence the drift to the Carlisle sheds of various Coronations during this period. Photograph W.A.C. Smith.

46247 CITY OF LIVERPOOL hurries up to Euston on the Up Fast through Watford Junction on 15 March 1961. The Watford DC electric lines (Bakerloo LT too, then) and its bays on the side of the station are depicted perfectly.

46247 CITY OF LIVERPOOL pauses at Stirling with the 10am Euston to Aberdeen, 31 August 1962. It had been a Camden engine all its life, from entering service in 1943 until the class began to disperse in the early 1960s. Since June 1961 it had been at Carlisle Kingmoor. Photograph W.A.C. Smith.

Under The Wires: 4. 46248 CITY OF LEEDS with the 11.45am Euston to Morecambe and Workington near Basford Hall, south of Crewe, 15 July 1961. The original CITY OF LEEDS had been 6244 of 1940; it had been renamed KING GEORGE VI in April 1941 and the original name had duly passed to 6248 on its building a couple of years later. Photograph Michael Mensing.

46248 CITY OF LEEDS in the blue livery (not that you'd really know it) starts the Mid-Day Scot out of Euston in August 1953. It entered Crewe Works a week or two later for a Heavy General and emerged in September/October with green livery, though it retained the sloping smokebox. Access to the steam pipes and so on for maintenance and repairs was obtained by removing the bolts on that oblong section of the deflectors above the cylinder and sliding it back. Photograph George Heiron, courtesy Mrs Shirley Heiron, The Transport Treasury.

The entry to traffic of 46249 CITY OF SHEFFIELD in April 1944 marked the reversion to conventional form for new locomotives, together with the running plate draped in front of the cylinders and the deflector extended down to match. This was the same for the batch 6249-6252. The open framing on the front reappeared with 6253-6257. In quite beautiful condition CITY OF SHEFFIELD (yet to get the 'cleaner's toecap' notch at the bottom of the deflector) stands at Upperby, in blue, 5 June 1952. Photograph J.L. Stevenson, courtesy Hamish Stevenson.

46250 CITY OF LICHFIELD on a late running Euston-Perth train, arriving at Stafford on 4 March 1961. Without wishing to labour the point, it is hard to resist yet again drawing attention to the prodigious load hanging on the engine. Photograph Michael Mensing.

46250 CITY OF LICHFIELD, a Carlisle Upperby engine by now (it had gone there in June 1958) at Shrewsbury, almost certainly off a fill-in turn from Crewe. Photograph Paul Chancellor Collection.

One of the traditionally nocturnal Crewe North 'big 'uns', 46251 CITY OF NOTTINGHAM (maroon since late 1958) on the ash pits at Camden on 28 April 1963. Photograph Malcolm S. Castledine.

A perfect CITY OF NOTTINGHAM, thoroughly bulled-up for the famous RCTS 'East Midlander' tour of 9 May 1964, stands at Didcot that day without, inexplicably, the headboard. The tour is best remembered for the memorable photographs published in the railway press at the time, of the Coronation standing at Swindon shed alongside 7022 HEREFORD CASTLE. Photograph Alec Swain, The Transport Treasury.

There would usually be something of a 'star' at Derby Works Open Day and a very appropriate one on 31 August 1963 was CITY OF NOTTINGHAM, then in its last full year of life. Anyone recognise themselves? Photograph Malcolm S. Castledine.

46252 CITY OF LEICESTER in green at Camden shed on 7 October 1962; AWS, electrification flashes. The sloping front to the running plate was not the only odd consequence of these engines being built conventionally rather than streamlined. As has already been touched upon, they also got 'semi-streamlined' tenders – when their construction began, it was thought they would be running behind streamlined engines. A feature to note is the water feed valve and 'sieve' box on the tender underframe between the leading and middle (or more properly 'intermediate') tender axles each side. They fed the exhaust steam and live steam injectors. It was a modification which dated from Ivatt's time (see his 2-6-0s and 2-6-2Ts and the BR Standards) and was subsequently applied to the rest of the class. Note the enormous quantity of coal in the tender. Photograph The Transport Treasury.

46252 CITY OF LEICESTER undergoing repair at Kingmoor, old style, with piston valves taken out using blocks and pulleys tied to the smokebox door handrail. CITY OF LEICESTER's valves and pistons are getting attention and the slidebars and connecting rods (though not the crossheads) have been taken off. The front vacuum pipe pushed to one side out of the way and the screw coupling is off to give access, leaving just the AWS protection plate. As Alec Swain noted in *British Railways Illustrated* Vol.11 No.12 (September 2002) in 'Carlisle Coronations': *That curious sack (they came from Crewe Works to shed stores full of newly made nuts and bolts) would hold the fitter's basic tools, to save the walk to and from the tool cupboard; others used a bucket, which had the additional advantage that it could serve as a wash basin at the end of the day, filled with hot water from the injector overflow on the nearest engine. Luxury! Note pit board, enough to give a present-day safety apparatchik the vapours.* Photograph The Transport Treasury.

46253 CITY OF ST ALBANS with the down Mid-Day Scot at Oxenholme, as usual with a train of inordinate length and taking Grayrigg (sixteen on at about 600 tons) without a banker. Note empty tender – she would come off at Carlisle! Photograph Locofotos.

46253
CITY OF ST ALBANS
46253

CITY OF STOKE-ON-TRENT

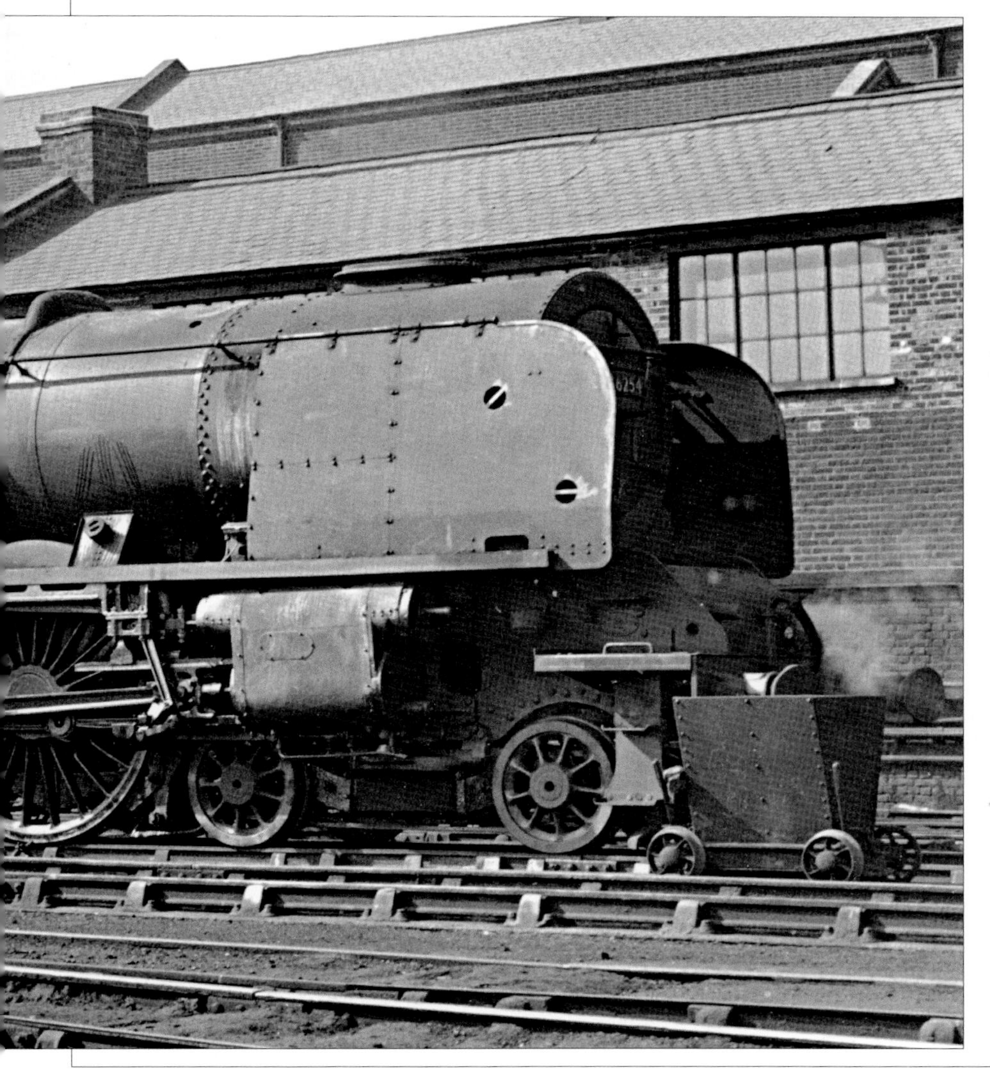

Top left. 46253 CITY OF ST ALBANS (the plate had little 'T' in the 'ST') at Polmadie on 13 September 1959. Photograph Alec Swain, The Transport Treasury.

Left. 46254 CITY OF STOKE-ON-TRENT (the nameplate dutifully uses the dashes) on the servicing roads at the south end of Camden shed about 1950. That tub is part of the ash handling and disposal system. Photograph The Transport Treasury.

Above. For two months in the spring of 1959 Glasgow Central station was closed on Sundays to allow resignalling work. Long distance trains were directed to Buchanan Street and services to and from the coast used St Enoch. On Sunday 3 May that year 46254 CITY OF STOKE-ON-TRENT, after passing Germiston Junction, is approaching Balornock on the climb from Buchanan Street with the up Mid-Day Scot. Photograph W.A.C. Smith.

46255 CITY OF HEREFORD in beautiful condition in the early 1950s – note early 'speedo' bracket by the rear driver, as on CITY OF LEEDS at Euston. Photograph Eric Treacy, NRM.

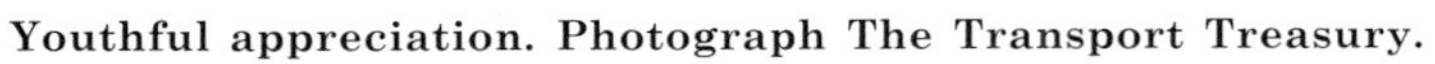
Youthful appreciation. Photograph The Transport Treasury.

46255 CITY OF HEREFORD waits departure from Stirling with the 8.35pm Sutton Coldfield car sleeper as Black Five 44999 approaches with a down freight, 31 July 1963. Photograph W.A.C. Smith.

1X82
46255
CITY OF HEREFORD
46255

1X82
S·L·S
SPECIAL

A Big 'Un On Tour

The Stephenson Locomotive Society ran a celebrated excursion from Birmingham on Sunday 12 July 1964, the 'Pennine Three Summits Railtour' utilising two Coronations with a Jubilee and a Royal Scot thrown in for good measure. The eleven coach special left New Street at 8.50am behind 46251 CITY OF NOTTINGHAM and ran on the LNW to Carlisle via Wolverhampton, Crewe, Warrington and Penrith. At Carlisle the special (extraordinarily as it might seem to us now) actually worked into Carlisle Kingmoor shed yard (and maybe even Upperby too – the SLS Journal report is silent on the details). These three pictures all show the Kingmoor part of this impressive tour. In the first picture (top left) the second Coronation, 46255 CITY OF HEREFORD, is standing in the shed yard ready for the second leg on to Leeds. The tour has 'landed' and the first participants are already making their way past the engine into the shed. In the second picture (below left) CITY OF HEREFORD has attached itself at the front of the 'Pennine Three Summits', the headboard has been transferred from 46251 (one – maybe the only – example of a top lamp iron being lowered on a Coronation) and the ensemble will soon be ready to leave. Britannias abounded in Carlisle by this time – in the background is one of them, 70009 ALFRED THE GREAT with, in between, a number of the brethren, including a somewhat bemused lady. Yearning for those days, we love the sort of happy ignorance of today's 'health n' safety' culture on display here: *a bloke sitting astride the main line to get his photograph.* The train left Kingmoor five minutes late 'although', the SLS Journal records dryly, 'it would have been less had it not been for delinquent customers'. CITY OF HEREFORD got its train to Leeds only four minutes late after being held at signals outside the station. Jubilee 45647 STURDEE made a brave fist of things from Leeds to Crewe despite a load of 400 tons over Standedge where the limit was 375 tons. The final leg from Crewe back to Birmingham produced 'one of the best steam times for some years', compliments of 46155 THE LANCER. The third picture (above) shows CITY OF HEREFORD leaving the loops alongside Kingmoor shed, faces at every window with, by now, a group of hangers-on straddling the main line (again) and yet another disgraceful instance of trespass on the abutment on the left. The sign up on the right no doubt warns of stern penalties awaiting errant trainspotters... First two photographs Alec Swain, The Transport Treasury; third one W.A.C. Smith.

That platform presence... 46255 CITY OF HEREFORD in green at Carlisle, northbound with the 1.44pm to Perth, which had left Crewe at 9.20pm. The coal in the tender is high, so it would have just come on from Upperby shed. The train was a leisurely one, the daytime Crewe-Perth which always had a 'big 'un' until their withdrawal at the end of the 1964 summer timetable. As Allan Baker commented in *British Railways Illustrated* Vol.10 No.6 (March 2001): *Four hours and 11 minutes were allowed between Crewe and Carlisle, with stops at all principal stations, and a plethora of connections to make. It was due in Perth at 5.20pm, and through coaches to Edinburgh were due at 3.56pm, and Inverness 9.35pm.* Photograph Dr Alan Roscoe, The Transport Treasury.

46256 SIR WILLIAM A. STANIER F.R.S. at Camden. Oddly, it took more than ten years to bring into service a class of just thirty-eight locomotives. The intention with the last two (the final one emerging as a BR locomotive) was to incorporate remedies to all the painful problems encountered in a decade of experience. Roller bearings throughout and manganese steel linings to the axleboxes and hornguides would, it was (vainly) hoped, raise mileages between shoppings to a totemic 100,000. Externally the last two were markedly different – note the cast steel Delta trailing truck, redesigned after some false starts to make room for the new rocking grate, together with hopper ashpan. The cab sides were different and the prominent new reverser presaged the way this feature would be arranged on the future BR Standards. Photograph The Transport Treasury.

Under The Wires: 5 and 6. Filthy and bestriped, SIR WILLIAM calls at Bletchley with an up express, 21 August 1964. Photographs Alec Swain, The Transport Treasury.

Above. SIR WILLIAM at Crewe North, 26 April 1964. The last two had this distinctive 'Delta' trailing truck – hence the cab side sheet cut off at the bottom, in order to accommodate it. The new design of truck also meant the AWS battery box was slung underneath the cab, on the left-hand side, so it's not visible here – it shows up well in the picture of 46257 at Shrewsbury shed in *Accompaniment:1*. The tender leading axle box has a mileage recorder, just visible as a projecting knob and, 'as exclusively revealed' in the said *Accompaniment:1* the last two, 46256 and 46257 had these mileage recorders, one each side. They presumably read forward running and rearward running separately. Insofar as anyone took any notice, you'd have to add the two together to divine the actual miles run. Looking this good, it seems almost lunacy that their withdrawal was already imminent. SIR WILLIAM (why the engine was not preserved is anybody's guess) had another minor claim to fame, for which we can thank long-time Irwell Press contributor, aide, advisor and dealer out of deserved stern rebukes Eric Youldon. For a while 46256 carried some equipment (similar to the familiar 'speedo' on the rear driver) adjacent to the leading left-hand bogie wheel, unique to this Pacific: *This was an experimental speedometer fitted in May 1951 at the instigation of Derby. The reason for it was the complaint from Drivers that the speedometer drive from the rear coupled wheel was unreliable at low speed on account of the low RPM of 6ft 9in drivers. This deficiency was important when negotiating speed restrictions, so a scheme was drawn up for a bogie wheel drive where revolutions were higher for a given speed and applied to No.46256. The generator was attached via a flexible connection to the front left-hand outside steamchest cover, and the cylinder drain pipes were extended forward and lowered so that any discharge was kept clear of the equipment. The existing speedometer was retained so presumably there were two dials in the cab. Rotation of the generator was obtained by means of a long tube threaded through the bogie wheel axle that was secured by a nut on the far side. The draughtsman responsible for the scheme (Dennis G. Monk) carrying out orders from high authority, had little faith in the experiment and doubted whether it would last 12 months! It was still in place in early 1958 although it is absent in views taken a few years later.* Photograph Frank Hornby.

Left. Carlisle meeting, 21 August 1961. Photograph The Transport Treasury.

Pacific in Distress

Detail views of the final Coronation, 46257 CITY OF SALFORD, obviously taken to record this minor front end damage (the scene is outside Polmadie Repair Shop). Some sort of low speed collision, it must have been a shock for the crew, unless it had been stabled at the time. In that case it would have been shock for the other crew... The date is not known, but the Upperby shedplate 12B indicates it is 1958 or after – a period confirmed by the fitting of AWS. It did indeed spend various short periods in for Casual Repairs in 1959 and 1960. The interesting point is that the electric lighting survived for at least this long. The last two had steam turbo generators for the electric lights (it can be seen fitted behind the smoke deflector) but unfamiliarity amongst the fitting staff, lack of spares and so on saw them eventually abandoned.

In September 1964 the Coronations disappeared from the West Coast main line and other than 46256 (booked for an RCTS Special at the end of the month) were out of service on 10 September 1964. There were tales of giving them further work on the Southern, Waterloo-Bournemouth but this, sadly, came to nought. A cause for infinite regret, because several of them might have ended up in Woodham's yard and we'd have been grateful for a few more, even knocked about a bit...